Bella's Wish

Love is Beautiful

By Lucie Cote Contente

Illustrations by Randini Sevevirathna

©2022 Lucie Cote Contente

No part of this book may be reproduced or transmitted in any form or by any means, electronic or mechanical, including photocopying, recording or by any information storage and retrieval system, without permission from the author, except for the case of quotations embodied in reviews.

Bella was smiling in her sleep while having a beautiful dream about a yellow butterfly. It was flying all around her like it was playing with her. It made her so happy. She wished she was a yellow butterfly and could fly anywhere she wanted.

When Bella woke up, her mom said she had a surprise. She told Bella they were going for a ride in the car to adopt a puppy and kitten. Bella was so excited, she started hopping around and that made her mom laugh.

When Bella and her mom arrived at the animal rescue building, they went inside and saw a lot of dogs and cats waiting to be adopted. Bella walked around with her mom and said hi to all the animals. They stopped in front of a grey kitten. He was so small with big blue eyes. He said, "Hi, my name is Kobi, what's yours?" Bella knew she had found her new brother.

Bella and her mom walked over to the puppies. One puppy came to the side of the gate and said, "Hi, my name is Penny, what's yours?" Bella knew she had found her new sister.

On the way home Bella sat in the back seat of the car with Kobi and Penny. She looked at them and already loved them. Every day Bella let them sleep with her, play with all her toys and even shared her food with them. Bella said to them, "Even though we all look different we are now a family with lots of love and love is beautiful. "

One day Bella, Penny and Kobi were playing in the back yard. Penny started digging a hole and found a purple stone. While they looked at it, the stone seemed to get brighter. Just then they saw a big yellow butterfly flying around them. Bella said to Penny and Kobi, "I wish I was a butterfly." Bella pushed the stone back in the hole with her paw and put the dirt back over it. Bella said, "We should leave the stone in the ground." They all started playing again with each other until they got tired and then went inside the house and off to bed.

When Penny and Kobi woke up the next day, Bella was not there. They looked around the house but couldn't find her. It was a sunny morning so they went outside to play with their toys. Penny looked up and saw a big yellow butterfly. Penny told Kobi to look up. Kobi looked up and saw so many different colored butterflies flying around with the big yellow butterfly.

The big yellow butterfly came down to Penny and landed on her head. Then it flew onto Kobi's head. They looked at the butterfly and Kobi said to Penny, "Do you remember what Bella said yesterday about her wish to be a butterfly right before she touched the purple stone?" Kobi asked, "Do you think the purple stone was a magic stone?"

The butterfly looked at Penny and Kobi and said, "Yes, it was a magical stone." Kobi asked, "Bella is that you?" Bella said, "Yes, I am finally a butterfly. Now I can fly anywhere I want. I will come back and visit you often. Be good to each other and listen to mom."

Bella flew away with the other butterflies. She looked back at them and said, "Always remember I love you Penny and Kobi, and love is beautiful." Penny and Kobi watched Bella fly away. They shouted, "Bella, we love you" and they both smiled knowing that Bella's wish finally came true.

Lucie Cote Contente has published:

Bella From the Farm
Bella Goes to the Spa
Bella's wish

Gluten and Gluten Free Cooking in Perfect Harmony
Gluten and Gluten Free Cooking in Perfect Harmony Take 2
Gluten and Gluten Free Cooking in Perfect Harmony Take 3

Visit the website
www.luciecotecontentebooks.com
For JJ, Alex and Colton

www.ingramcontent.com/pod-product-compliance
Lightning Source LLC
Chambersburg PA
CBHW041408160426
42811CB00103B/1549